W9-AKU-986

To:-
From:-

Other Helen Exley Giftbooks:

Happy Anniversary
Merry Christmas
To a very Special Dad
To a very Special Daughter
To a very Special Friend
To a very Special Granddaughter
To a very Special Grandmother
To a very Special Grandpa
To a very Special Grandson
To a very Special Mother

To a very Special Sister
To a very Special Son
To a very Special Teacher
To my very Special Husband
To my very Special Wife
Welcome to the New Baby
Wishing You Happiness
To a Special Couple on your
   Wedding Day

Published simultaneously in 1992 by Exley Publications Ltd,
16 Chalk Hill, Watford, Herts WD1 4BN, in the United Kingdom,
and Exley Publications LLC, 232 Madison Avenue, Suite 1206,
NY 10016, in the USA.

24 23 22 21 20 19 18 17 16 15

Copyright © Helen Exley 1992
The moral right of the author has been asserted.
ISBN 1-85015-282-9
A copy of the CIP data is available from the British Library on request.
Printed in Hungary.

To my very special

LOVE

Illustrations by Juliette Clarke
A Helen Exley Giftbook

I wonder, by my troth, what you and I

Did, till we lov'd?

JOHN DONNE (1572 - 1631)

· · ·

≡EXLEY
NEW YORK • WATFORD, UK

Our love is like the misty
rain that falls softly - but
floods the river.
AFRICAN PROVERB

. . .

Love comforteth like
sunshine after rain.
WILLIAM SHAKESPEARE
(1564 - 1616)

. . .

Your love is comfort in
sadness, quietness in tumult,
rest in weariness,
hope in despair.
MARION C. GARRETTY, b.1917

. . .

OUR GENTLE LOVE

The touch of your hand in passing, so light, so swift,

that no one else suspects its loving reassurance -

that touch sustains me through the hardest day.

MARION C. GARRETTY, b. 1917

. . .

The hours I spend with you I look upon as a sort of

perfumed garden, a dim twilight, and a fountain

singing to it...you and you *alone* make me feel that I

am alive.... Other men it is said have seen angels,

but I have seen thee and thou art enough.

GEORGE MOORE (1852 - 1933)

. . .

Cherish me with that dignified tenderness

which I have only found in you...

MARY WOLLSTONECRAFT (1759 - 1797)
to Gilbert Imlay

. . .

Gladly I'll live in a poor mountain hut,

Spin, sew, and till the soil in any weather,

And wash in the cold mountain stream, if but

We dwell together.

JAPANESE LYRIC

. . .

<u>ALL FOR YOU</u>

Had I the heavens' embroidered cloths,

Enwrought with golden and silver light,

The blue and the dim and the dark cloths

Of night and light and the half-light,

I would spread the cloths under your feet:

But I, being poor, have only my dreams;

I have spread my dreams under your feet;

Tread softly because you tread on my dreams.

WILLIAM BUTLER YEATS (1865 - 1939)

. . .

I kiss your hands and kneel before you ... to assure
you that my whole mind, all the breadth of my
spirit, all my heart exist only to love you. I adore
you ... so beautiful, so perfect, so made to be
cherished, adored and loved to death and madness.

PRINCESS CAROLYNE JEANNE ELISABETH
VON SAYNWITTGENSTEIN

from *a letter to Liszt, circa 1847*

. . .

To me you are the gate of paradise. For you I will renounce fame, creativity, everything.

FREDERICK CHOPIN (1810 - 1849)
to his mistress Delphine Potocka

. . .

GREAT TRIBUTES

You are always new. The last of your kisses was ever
the sweetest; the last smile the brightest; the last
movement the gracefullest.

JOHN KEATS (1795 - 1821)
to Fanny Brawne

. . .

If I could write the beauty of your eyes
And in fresh numbers number all your graces,
The age to come would say, "This poet lies;
Such heavenly touches ne'er touch'd earthly faces."

WILLIAM SHAKESPEARE (1564 - 1616)

. . .

I could die for you. My creed is love and you are its
only tenet. You have ravish'd me away by power I
cannot resist.... I cannot breathe without you.

JOHN KEATS (1795 - 1821)
in a letter to Fanny Brawne

. . .

COMFORT AND SUPPORT

Love from one to another can only be that two

solitudes come nearer, recognize and

protect and comfort each other.

HAN SUYIN

. . .

Though it rains,

I won't get wet:

I'll use your love

For an umbrella.

JAPANESE FOLK SONG

. . .

In the huge mysteries of time

and space I feel your arm

about my shoulder and

am not afraid.

PAM BROWN, b.1928

. . .

You are always there for me and so you give
me the courage to stand alone.

MARION C. GARRETTY, b.1917

. . .

The supreme happiness of life is the
conviction of being loved for yourself,
or, more correctly, being loved
in spite of yourself.

VICTOR HUGO (1802 - 1885)

. . .

Love is simple to understand if you haven't
got a mind soft and full of holes. It's a crutch,
that's all, and there isn't one of us doesn't
need a crutch.

NORMAN MAILER, b.1923
from *"Barbary Shore"*

. . .

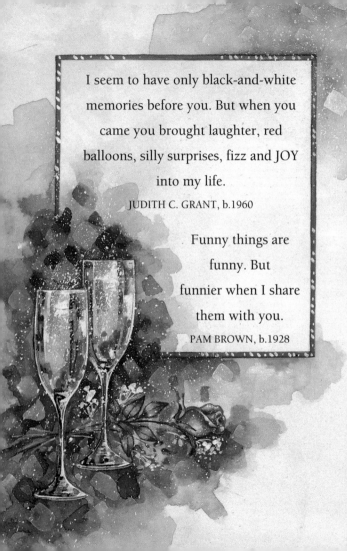

I seem to have only black-and-white memories before you. But when you came you brought laughter, red balloons, silly surprises, fizz and JOY into my life.

JUDITH C. GRANT, b.1960

Funny things are funny. But funnier when I share them with you.

PAM BROWN, b.1928

MAGIC MEMORIES

We take our own magic with us you and I.

Do you remember the bed that sagged like a

hammock, the room in Antwerp next to the

toilets, the Irish bedroom thick

with agonizing saints?

Do you remember the windows that overlooked

the brothel? The raggazzi revving bikes

under our balcony till dawn?

The frogs? The drains?

The door that wouldn't open? The shower we

couldn't stop? The landlady with the glass eye?

Strange breakfasts. Stranger suppers. Mice.

Do you remember the night when I laughed

myself out of bed?

All magic.

All memories to treasure all our days.

PAM BROWN, b.1928

. . .

A DEDICATION TO LOVE

Set me as a seal upon thine heart, as a seal upon
thine arm; for love is strong as death; jealousy is
cruel as the grave; the coals thereof are coals of fire,
which hath a most vehement flame. Many waters
cannot quench love, neither can the floods drown it.

from *"Solomon's Song"*

. . .

To love is to take the greatest risk of all.
It is to give one's future and one's happiness
into another's hands.
It is to allow oneself to trust without reserve.
It is to accept vulnerability.
And thus I love you.

HELEN THOMSON, b.1943

. . .

You could give yourself to another, but none could love you more purely or more completely than I did. To none could your happiness be holier, as it was to me, and always will be. My whole experience, everything that lives within me, everything, my most precious, I devote to you, and if I try to enoble myself, this is done in order to become ever worthier of you, to make you even happier.

JOHANN CHRISTOPH FRIEDRICH VON SCHILLER
(1759 - 1805)

to Lotte von Lengefeld

. . .

I love thee with the breath,
Smiles, tears, of all my life!

ELIZABETH BARRETT BROWNING (1806 - 1861)

ALWAYS THERE FOR ME

I love you for the smallest things; bluebells on my desk, a pat on the head when I made an awful speech, a cup of tea in the middle of a deadline panic, being the only one to tell me that the green skirt really does make me look like a sack of potatoes.

And the big things; giving me all the best things in your life, sharing my joys, being kind to me in all my failings and giving me courage.

HELEN THOMSON, b. 1943

. . .

Whenever I've needed someone to share my joy, or someone to hold me when my world rips to pieces, you're there. And I know you will be - tomorrow, always.

MAYA V. PATEL, b.1943

We are busy people, you and I. To accomplish what we do, we have to stave off all distractions and give up many special pleasures for the work we do. But our love is always there. True. Constant. Sure. Success or failure will hardly touch me if our venture falls apart at the seams. You will be there.

JESSE O'NEILL

. . .

Those days of freedom can be anywhere. Long silver beaches. Tangled alleyways. Temples against the skyline... churches resonant with song. Merry go rounds. Coral reefs. A rambling *pension* in Provence. But always at the heart of them a quiet room, high ceilinged, bright with sunlight, a great white bed. And you.

PAM BROWN, b.1928

. . .

All that I love loses half its pleasure if you
are not there to share it.

CLARA ORTEGA, b.1955

. . .

It's nice for me to be me,
It's nice for you to be you,
But it's best for us to be us.

PAM BROWN, b.1928

. . .

TOGETHER

To get the full value of joy you must have someone to divide it with.

MARK TWAIN (1835 - 1910)

. . .

I'd rather face failure with you beside me than success with anyone else.

JENNY DE VRIES (1947 - 1991)

. . .

When two people love each other, they don't look at each other, they look in the same direction.

GINGER ROGERS

. . .

To lie with you under a ceiling bright with shifting water shadows - that's good.
To drowse in flower-scented darkness - that's good.
But best of all is rain - drumming, roaring, gushing from the guttering - and we two warm and dry and safe together, in each other's arms.

PAM BROWN, b.1928

MISSING YOU

When you have gone away,

No flowers more, methinks, will be -

No maple leaves in all the world -

Till you come back to me.

YANAGIWARA YASU-KO (1783 - 1866)

. . .

Please suggest a remedy to stop me trembling with joy like a lunatic when I receive and read your letters.... You have given me a gift such as I never even dreamt of finding in this life.

FRANZ KAFKA (1883 - 1924)

. . .

The heap of blankets on our bed, the squash shirts hanging on the door, your tools on the kitchen table, the smell of your toothpaste.
Memories. Good memories. Touches of you that stay in our home and keep me close whenever you are gone.

HELEN THOMSON, b.1943

. . .

Even nights when I sleep alone
I set the pillows side by side:
One is my love -
Holding it close, I sleep.

JAPANESE FOLK SONG

. . .

EVERYTHING TO ME

For love, all love of other sights controls

And makes one little room, an everywhere.

JOHN DONNE (1572 - 1631)

. . .

Your words dispel all the care in the world

and make me happy... They are as

necessary to me now as sunlight and air...

Your words are my food, your breath

my wine - you are everything to me.

SARAH BERNHARDT (1844 - 1923)

. . .

Love is not to be reason'd down, or lost

In high ambition or a thirst of greatness;

'Tis second life, it grows into the soul

Warms every vein, and beats in every pulse.

JOSEPH ADDISON (1672 - 1719)

. . .

It is a short word, but it contains all:
it means the body, the soul, the life,
the entire being. We feel it as we feel the
warmth of the blood, we breathe it as we
breathe the air, we carry it in ourselves as
we carry our thoughts. Nothing more
exists for us. It is not a word; it is an
inexpressible state indicated by
four letters....

GUY DE MAUPASSANT (1850 - 1893)

. . .

...if we never met again in our lives I should
feel that somehow the whole adventure of
existence was justified by my having met
you.

LEWIS MUMFORD (1895 - 1990)
to his wife

. . .

YOUR GIFT TO ME

You give me thoughtful gifts - sugar almonds, a Vivaldi album, white home-grown chrysanthemums for my bedside table, a surprise walk through the bluebell woods. But the best thing is when I surprise you deep at work or you spot me in a crowd and your eyes light up with pleasure. For me, the best thing is to know how much you love me.

HELEN EXLEY

. . .

There is only one happiness in life, to love and be loved.

GEORGE SAND (AURORE DUDEVANT)

Two things cannot alter,

Since Time was, nor today:

The flowing of water;

And Love's strange, sweet way.

JAPANESE LYRIC

. . .

Love, all alike, no season knows, nor clime

Nor hours, days, months, which are

the rags of time.

JOHN DONNE (1572 - 1631)
from *"The Sun Rising"*

. . .

Until you're a hundred,

Until I'm ninety-nine,

Together

Until white hair grows

JAPANESE FOLK SONG

FOREVER

Doubt thou the stars are fire;

Doubt that the sun doth move;

Doubt truth to be a liar;

But never doubt I love.

WILLIAM SHAKESPEARE (1564 - 1616)

. . .

Any time that is not spent on love

is wasted.

TASSO (1544 - 1595)

. . .

Sensual pleasure passes and vanishes in the
twinkling of an eye, but the friendship between us,
the mutual confidence, the delights of the heart, the
enchantment of the soul, these things do not perish
and can never be destroyed. I shall love

you until I die.

VOLTAIRE (1694 - 1778)

to Mme. Denis

. . .